The Life of Jesus

in Masterpieces of Art

The Life of Jesus
in Masterpieces of Art

⚜

Mary Pope Osborne

VIKING

Author's Note

In my retelling of the life of Jesus, I have tried to be as clear and direct as possible, without sacrificing the wonder and passion of the story. That task has been greatly helped by the works of a number of European painters.

At the end of the sixth century, Pope Gregory the Great said, "Painting can do for the illiterate what writing does for those who can read." Consequently, in the centuries that followed, the artists of western Europe were encouraged to use their imaginations to portray the stories in the Gospels. Since most people could not read, they learned about the life of Jesus through paintings, sculpture, and stained glass windows.

Many of the masterpieces included in this book were painted in the fifteenth and sixteenth centuries during the Renaissance, when western religious art reached unparalleled heights of beauty and inspiration. Works by Botticelli, Fra Angelico, van der Weyden, and others show how painting was beginning to reflect real life. Renaissance artists developed the science of perspective, which gave their paintings an illusion of depth. Also, while staying true to Biblical characters and events, they painted the clothing and scenery of their contemporary culture. As a result, events in the life of Jesus felt immediate and personal to the onlooker.

I am deeply grateful to these master painters for helping me tell the story that has been told again and again—the story that has profoundly influenced world culture for the last two thousand years.

—M. P. O.

Two thousand years ago, the Jewish regions of Judea and Galilee on the eastern Mediterranean were ruled by the Romans. Jewish prophets had written that God would someday send a Messiah, or savior, to his people. Many Jews prayed for the Messiah to come and rescue them from their Roman oppressors.

Long ago, in a city of Galilee called Nazareth, there

lived a young Jewish woman named Mary. Mary was engaged to marry Joseph, a kind man who worked as a carpenter. But one day when Mary was alone, the angel Gabriel appeared before her. "Hail, favored one," the angel said, "the Lord is with you."

Mary was so startled that at first she could not speak.

"Fear not, Mary," the angel said, "for you have found favor with God. Soon you shall bear a son, and you shall call him Jesus."

"How can this be?" said Mary. "I am not yet married."

"The Holy Spirit will come to you," said the angel. "The power of the Most High will overshadow you, and the child who is born will be the Son of God."

"Let it be according to your word," Mary whispered. And the angel departed from her.

When Joseph found out that Mary was going to have a baby, he planned to break his engagement with her. But the angel Gabriel appeared to him in a dream. "Take Mary to be your wife," he said, "for the father of her child is the Holy Spirit. Soon she shall give birth to a son, and you shall name him Jesus, and he shall be the savior of his people."

Joseph did as the angel told him and took Mary to be his wife. Months later, the Roman Emperor Augustus sent forth a decree that all the people in the empire must return to their home cities to be registered for taxation. Though Mary's child was soon to be born, she and Joseph left Galilee and traveled south to Bethlehem, the home of Joseph's ancestors.

When they arrived in the crowded city, they found no room at the inn and were forced to seek shelter in a stable.

While they were staying in the stable, the baby was born to Mary. She wrapped him in swaddling clothes and made him a bed in a manger.

⚜

In a nearby field, shepherds were keeping watch over their flocks.

Suddenly an angel stood before them, and they were terrified.

"Behold, I bring you good tidings of great joy," the angel said. "Unto you is born a savior, which is Christ the Lord. You shall find him in Bethlehem lying in a manger."

A multitude of angels then appeared, praising God. "Glory to God in the highest," they said, "and on earth peace, good will toward men."

The shepherds hurried to Bethlehem where they found the baby in the manger. They told Mary and Joseph all that they had seen and heard.

After Jesus was born, wise men from

the East arrived in Jerusalem, the holy city of Judea. They went to Herod, the king of Judea, and said, "Where is the baby born to be king of the Jews? We have seen his star in the East and have come to worship him."

Herod was greatly disturbed by this news, for he feared that a newborn king might someday threaten his power. He gathered his priests and scribes together and asked them about this child.

"We have read in the scripture that a leader of the Jews is to be born in Bethlehem," they told him.

Herod sent the wise men to Bethlehem and asked them to bring him word when they had found the infant, so that he, too, could go and worship him. In truth, Herod planned to kill Jesus.

A star in the East led the wise men on to Bethlehem. When they found the baby Jesus, they knelt before him and worshiped him, then opened their treasure chests and gave him great gifts of gold, frankincense, and myrrh.

The wise men were warned in a dream not to return to King Herod, so they returned to their own country by another way.

 When Herod discovered that
the wise men had betrayed him,
he went into a rage and ordered his soldiers
to hurry to Bethlehem and slay all children two years old and
under. But before Herod's men arrived, an angel appeared to Joseph in a

dream. "Take the child and flee to Egypt," the angel said, "for Herod intends to murder him."

Joseph rose at once, and he and Mary fled into the night with their baby. They lived in Egypt until they received news of Herod's death. Then the family traveled back to Nazareth together.

Every year, Mary and Joseph went to Jerusalem

for the Jewish festival of Passover. When Jesus was twelve years old, he made the journey with them.

Returning home after the festival, Mary and Joseph discovered that Jesus was missing from their group. They hurried back to Jerusalem, and after three days of frantic searching, they found him in the temple.

Jesus was sitting with the religious teachers, asking and answering difficult questions. The teachers all seemed astonished at Jesus' understanding of spiritual teachings.

"Son, why have you treated us this way?" said Mary. "For three days, your father and I have been searching for you."

"Why were you searching for me?" said Jesus. "Did you not know that you could find me in my Father's house?"

❧

Jesus then returned with Mary and Joseph to Nazareth, and in the years to come, he grew wise and strong, and God was pleased with him.

Eighteen years later, a prophet called John the

Baptist began preaching in the wilderness of Judea.

John ate only locusts and wild honey and wore clothes made of camel hair. He proclaimed that the savior of the Jews would soon arrive, and to prepare for his coming, all people needed to be baptized – washed clean of their sins.

⚜

When Jesus was thirty, he left Galilee and went to the river Jordan to be baptized by John.

As soon as John saw Jesus, he realized that this man was the savior for whom he had been waiting. "Behold the Lamb of God, who takes away the sins of the world!" he cried.

⚜

When John baptized Jesus, the sky parted and the spirit of God descended like a dove down upon Jesus, and a voice from Heaven said, "This is my beloved Son, with whom I am well pleased."

After Jesus was baptized, he traveled alone into the

desert to pray and think about God.

For forty days and forty nights he went without food. When he was suffering from great hunger, the devil came to him to tempt him. "If you are the Son of God," the devil said, "command that these stones be turned into bread."

"A person does not live by bread alone," Jesus said, "but also by the words that come from the mouth of God."

The devil then led Jesus to the top of a temple and told him to hurl himself down and let the angels rescue him.

Jesus refused. "It is wrong to test God's power," he said.

The devil led Jesus to a high mountain and showed him all the riches of the kingdoms of the world. "If you bow down and worship me," he said, "I will give you all this."

"Get away from me, Satan!" said Jesus. "For it is written that a person must worship God and serve only him."

Jesus left the desert and returned to Nazareth in Galilee to begin his ministry. "God has sent me to heal the brokenhearted," he told a crowd, "to preach freedom to slaves, and to give sight to the blind."

Many people were amazed at the wonderful things Jesus said. His teachings were called the gospel, which means "good news."

But some people grew angry with him. "What power does he have?" they asked. "Is he not just the son of a carpenter?"

His enemies grew so angry that they threatened to throw Jesus off a cliff. But he slipped away from the crowd and left Nazareth.

As he traveled about Galilee, preaching to the people, his fame grew, and many gathered to hear him. One day near a lake, when a great crowd pressed upon him, he climbed into a fishing boat and preached to the people on the shore. After the crowd had left, Jesus told the owners of the boat, Simon and Andrew, to cast their net into the lake.

"Master, we have been fishing all night and caught nothing," the two brothers said.

Nevertheless, Simon and Andrew did as Jesus told them. Soon their net was filled with so many fish that it began to break, and they had to call to their partners, John and James, for help.

The four fishermen were astonished by their great catch. "Fear not," Jesus said to them. "From now on, you shall catch men."

Simon (whom Jesus named Peter), Andrew, John, and James became Jesus' first disciples. They began traveling with him throughout Galilee as he preached the gospel. They watched him heal the diseases and afflictions of those who came to him.

One day Jesus and his disciples arrived at a wedding feast in the town of Cana. When they discovered that there was no more wine, Jesus told the servants of the house to fill six stone jars with water and take them into the feast. The servants did as he commanded and soon discovered that their jars held many gallons of wine.

When his disciples witnessed this miracle, they believed in Jesus even more.

Over time, Jesus chose
twelve disciples to help him in his work. To them he gave the power to heal, and he called them "apostles" which means "those who are sent out."

People began to follow Jesus and his disciples from town to town to see his miracles and to hear his wisdom. One day when a great crowd had gathered to hear him, Jesus went up on a mountain and taught some of his wisest lessons:

"Blessed are the poor in spirit: for theirs is the kingdom of heaven.

"Blessed are they that mourn: for they shall be comforted.

"Blessed are the meek: for they shall inherit the earth.

"Blessed are they which do hunger and thirst after righteousness:
for they shall be filled.

"Blessed are the merciful: for they shall obtain mercy.

"Blessed are the pure in heart: for they shall see God.

"Blessed are the peacemakers: for they shall be called the children of God.

"Blessed are they which are persecuted for righteousness' sake:
for theirs is the kingdom of heaven.

"Blessed are ye, when men shall revile you, and persecute you,
and shall say all manner of evil against you falsely, for my sake.

"Rejoice, and be exceeding glad, for great is your reward in heaven."

That day, in this Sermon on the Mount, Jesus said, "Whatever you wish others would do for you, do for them." And he taught that people should love their enemies as well as their friends. He said that only if people forgive others will God forgive them.

Jesus also taught his followers a prayer called "The Lord's Prayer": *Our Father which art in heaven, Hallowed be thy name. Thy kingdom come, Thy will be done in earth, as it is in heaven. Give us this day our daily bread. And forgive us our debts, as we forgive our debtors. And lead us not into temptation, but deliver us from evil: For thine is the kingdom, and the power, and the glory, for ever. Amen.*

Jesus' fame spread throughout the land. As

more people wanted to hear him, he sent his disciples out to spread his message. One day when all had returned, he took them to a secluded spot to rest.

But soon people heard that Jesus was nearby, and they hurried to see him, until there was a throng of five thousand. Jesus felt such compassion for them that he spent the whole day teaching them.

When evening came, his disciples urged him to send the crowd into nearby villages to buy food for dinner.

"How much food is here?" Jesus asked.

"There are only five loaves of bread and two fishes, belonging to a small boy," the disciples said.

Jesus blessed the boy's loaves of bread and two fishes. Then he told the disciples to give them to the crowd.

Miraculously, the boy's food multiplied until all five thousand people were fed. There was even enough left over to fill twelve large baskets.

After Jesus had fed the crowd, he asked his disciples to leave him. He wanted to be alone to pray.

The disciples departed in a boat. During the night, a storm came up at sea, and the boat tossed on the water. In the early hours of the morning, they saw an incredible sight: Jesus was coming toward them.

He was walking on the water.

His disciples cried out in fear, for they thought they were seeing a ghost. "It is I," Jesus called to them. "Be not afraid."

"Lord, if it really is you," said Peter, "tell me to come to you on the water."

"Come," said Jesus.

Peter got out of the boat and started walking across the water. But when he felt the wind, he became afraid and began to sink.

"Save me, Lord!" he cried.

Jesus stretched forth his hand and caught Peter. "O you of little faith," he said, "why did you doubt?"

When Peter and Jesus were safe in the boat, the wind ceased, and everyone praised and worshiped Jesus. "Truly you are the Son of God," they said.

One day when Jesus was teaching,

he reminded people that they should love their neighbor as they loved themselves.

"But who is my neighbor?" asked a listener.

Jesus then told the parable of a Jewish man traveling to the city of Jericho. On his way, the man was attacked by thieves and left for dead.

A priest passed by him and ignored him. Then another man passed by him without stopping.

Soon a Samaritan came by. Jews and Samaritans did not mix with each other, but when the Samaritan saw the bleeding man, he decided to help him. He bandaged his wounds and led him to an inn, where he took good care of him.

"Which was the man's real neighbor?" Jesus asked.

"The one who showed pity," the crowd said.

Jesus told them to go and do as the good Samaritan had done.

⚜

Another day, when a great multitude had gathered to hear Jesus speak, the scribes and Pharisees looked at the people with disgust, for many appeared to be poor sinners and outcasts.

Sensing the scorn of these religious leaders, Jesus explained that the angels felt great joy whenever any sinner repented. Then he told a parable about the prodigal son:

A father once divided his property between two sons. The older stayed at home. But the younger journeyed into a far country, where he wasted all his money and lived foolishly.

When famine overtook the land, the younger son found himself starving. He was forced to eat the food that the pigs ate in the farmyard. Filled with regret and sorrow, he decided to return home and beg forgiveness from his father.

From a long way off, the father saw his younger son coming home, and he joyfully ran to greet him.

"Father, I have sinned against heaven and before you," the young man said. "I am not worthy to be called your son."

But the happy father bid his servants to prepare a great feast for his prodigal son. The older son complained, saying he had always served his father well, but had never been given a feast.

"Son, you are always with me," said the father, "and all I have is yours. But we must celebrate, for your brother was dead and now is alive. He was lost and now is found."

In a village one day, as Jesus was teaching, a group of small children tried to get close to him. His disciples moved quickly to keep the children away, but Jesus stopped them.

"Let them come to me," he said, "for the kingdom of God belongs to those who are like children." Then Jesus took them in his arms and blessed them.

Jesus had three close friends who lived in the town of Bethany in Judea. They were Lazarus and his sisters, Mary and Martha.

When Jesus heard that Lazarus was very ill, he wanted to go to him. His disciples told him that his enemies in Judea might try to seize him. But Jesus ignored their warnings and hurried to the home of Lazarus.

When he arrived, he discovered that his friend had been dead for four days. "Lord, if you had been here, my brother would not have died!" cried Martha.

"Your brother shall rise again," said Jesus. "I am the resurrection and the life. He who believes in me, though he were dead, yet shall he live."

Jesus ordered that the tomb be opened. He

prayed to his Father; then he called out, "Lazarus, come forth." And Lazarus rose from the dead.

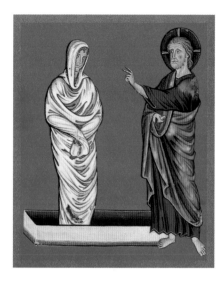

After this miracle, Jesus' fame became so great that the chief priests and scribes met in a council. "What can we do?" they asked fearfully. "If we do nothing, everyone will believe what he says is true." From that day on, they plotted how they could arrest Jesus and put him to death.

When the festival of Passover drew near,

many in Jerusalem waited excitedly for Jesus to arrive. Drawing close to the city, Jesus asked two disciples to bring him a donkey to ride.

As he rode the donkey, people laid their garments in his path and waved palm leaves.

"Hosanna!" they shouted. "Blessed is the King of Israel that comes in the name of the Lord!"

When he arrived at the temple of Jerusalem, Jesus was furious to find it filled with moneychangers and people selling pigeons, sheep, and oxen. He overthrew the tables and scattered the money. "My Father's house is a house of prayer," he said. "But you have turned it into a den of thieves."

Jesus' enemies were afraid to arrest him before a crowd. But soon a man came to them and offered to betray Jesus. The man was one of Jesus' own disciples: Judas Iscariot. In exchange for thirty pieces of silver, Judas promised to deliver Jesus to his enemies when he was alone.

On the night of Passover, Jesus and his disciples gathered for supper in the upper room of a house.

In the course of the evening, Jesus blessed the bread and broke it, and

he gave a piece to each of his disciples. "Take and eat," he said. "This is my body."

Then he passed a cup of wine around the table. "Take and drink," he said. "This is my blood."

As they were eating, Jesus told his disciples that one of them would soon betray him.

"Is it I?" "Is it I?" the disciples asked, but Jesus would not say.

"Lord, who is he?" Peter whispered.

"The one to whom I now give this bread," Jesus answered, and he handed a piece of bread to Judas Iscariot. "What you must do, do quickly," he said.

Judas left the table and hurried out into the night to meet with Jesus' enemies.

Jesus then told his disciples that he was soon going to leave them.

"Lord, where will you go?" asked Peter.

"Where I am going, you cannot follow me now," said Jesus.

"But why?" said Peter. "I would lay down my life for you."

"Will you lay down your life for me, Peter?" Jesus asked his dearest disciple. "Before the rooster crows, you will deny three times that you even know me."

 The apostles sang a hymn with Jesus and followed him out of the upper room into the night. He took Peter, John, and James with him into a garden called Gethsemane. He asked them to stay awake with him, for he was deeply sad.

He knelt in the garden and prayed, "Father, all things are possible to thee. Let this cup pass from me. Yet, do Thy will, not mine."

Three times Jesus found his disciples had fallen asleep, and three times he woke them. The third time, he said, "The hour has come."

A moment later, Judas Iscariot led a band of soldiers into the garden. They carried lanterns, torches, and weapons. Judas had told them to arrest the man whom he kissed.

"Hail, Master," said Judas, and he kissed Jesus.

The soldiers seized Jesus. As they led him away, all his disciples fled, except Peter who followed at a distance.

Jesus was taken to the house of the high priest where soldiers blindfolded him, beat him, and mocked him.

As Peter watched from the courtyard, a servant girl pointed at him. "You were with Jesus," she said.

Peter was fearful. "I do not know what you mean," he said.

Another maid pointed at Peter and said, "This man was with Jesus of Nazareth." Again, Peter denied that it was true.

When a third person accused Peter of knowing Jesus, he insisted even more fervently that he did not.

At that moment, the rooster crowed, and Peter remembered Jesus' words: *Before the rooster crows, you will deny three times that you even know me.*

Peter ran from the courtyard and wept with shame.

Jesus' tormentors bound him and brought him before Pilate, the governor from Rome. "I find no reason to accuse this man," Pilate said.

But his enemies insisted that Jesus had stirred up crowds from Galilee to Judea.

"What do you wish me to do with him?" asked Pilate.

"Let him be crucified!" they said.

"Why? What evil has he done?" said Pilate.

But they shouted all the more, "Let him be crucified!"

Pilate washed his hands. "I am innocent of this man's blood," he said. Then he had Jesus beaten and handed him over to the crowd.

The soldiers put a scarlet robe on Jesus and twisted some thorns into a crown and placed it on his head. They mocked him, then led him away to be crucified.

❧ 37 ❧

Jesus was taken to a place called Golgotha. He was

nailed to a cross; and above his head was a sign that read: *This is Jesus, the King of the Jews.*

"Father, forgive them, for they know not what they do," said Jesus.

Watching from a distance were some women who loved Jesus. His mother Mary and his friend Mary Magdalene grieved as they saw him dying upon the cross.

At noon, darkness came over the earth and lasted until three o'clock. At that hour, Jesus cried out, "My God, my God, why hast thou forsaken me?"

The soldiers mocked him and gave him vinegar to drink.

Then Jesus said in a loud voice, "Father, into Thy hands I commit my spirit!" And he breathed his last breath.

At once the earth shook, and rocks split apart. A Roman officer guarding Jesus was astonished by what he saw. "Truly this man was the Son of God," he said.

The body of Jesus was taken down from the cross. It was wrapped in a clean linen shroud and laid in a tomb.

Two days later, on Sunday, Mary Magdalene came to the

tomb early in the morning, while it was still dark. When she saw that the stone in front of the tomb had been rolled back, she ran to tell Peter and John.

"They have taken our Lord, and I do not know where they have laid him!" she said.

The two disciples ran with Mary to the tomb. They found the linen cloths, but not the body of Jesus. They did not understand what had happened, so they returned home, leaving Mary Magdalene to mourn alone.

While she was grieving, she saw two angels sitting where the body of Jesus had been. The angels asked her why she was weeping.

"Because they have taken away my Lord," she said, "and I do not know where they have laid him."

As she spoke, she turned and saw a man standing nearby. "Woman, why are you weeping? Whom do you seek?" he asked.

Through her tears, Mary mistook him for a gardener. "Tell me where you have laid him," she said, "and I will take him away."

"Mary," the man said simply.

Suddenly she knew the man was Jesus. "Master!" she cried.

"Go to my disciples," he said to her, "and tell them that I am going to my Father and your Father, to my God and your God."

Mary Magdalene ran to the disciples and told them that she had seen Jesus, and she told them what he had said.

Not long afterward, when the eleven remaining apostles were gathered in Jerusalem, Jesus appeared before them. They cried out in fear, thinking he was a ghost.

He tried to calm them. "Why are you troubled? See my hands and my feet," he said. "A spirit has not flesh and bones as I have."

The apostles were overjoyed, and they gave Jesus fish and honeycomb to eat.

"Go now into all the world," he told them, "and preach to all nations, baptizing them in the name of the Father, the Son, and the Holy Ghost. Teach them to observe all the things I have commanded you, and know that I am with you, even unto the end of the world."

Jesus led his apostles as far as Bethany; then he lifted up his hands and blessed them. And while he blessed them, he was parted from them and carried up to his Father in heaven.

His apostles returned to Jerusalem with great joy. Soon they would go out into the world and tell the story of Jesus Christ.

THE PICTURES

The Virgin Teaching the Infant Jesus to Read by Sandro Botticelli (1444/5–1510)

Madonna and Child by William H. Patten (d.1843)

Annunciation Bruges or Ghent Hastings Hours, c.1480

The Visitation from The Hours of Marshal Jean de Boucicaut, (Use of Paris) Boucicaut Hours, early fifteenth century

Annunciation to the Shepherds, from The Coeting Hours by the Coeting Master (1450–75)

Mystic Nativity by Sandro Botticelli (1444/5–1510)

Adoration of the Magi, Bourges Tilliot Hours, late fifteenth century

Meeting of the Magi by the Limbourg brothers, Très Riches Heures du Duc de Berry, early fifteenth century

The Massacre of the Innocents by Fra Angelico (c.1387–1455)

Flight into Egypt, c.1525,
French School

*Presentation of the Infant Jesus in
the Temple,* by the Master of
Osma, Breviary of the Bishop of
Montoya,1460

Christ Among the Doctors by
Bonifazio Veronese (de Pitati)
(1487–1553)

*The Twelve-year-old Jesus in the
Temple* by the Second Master of
Aranyosmarot (*fl.c.*1460)

Baptism of Christ by Francesco
Ubertini Bacchiacca, II
(1494–1557)

John Baptizing Jesus,
Archbishop Chichele's
Breviary, early fifteenth century

*The Holy Family with Saint
Elizabeth and the Infant John the
Baptist* by Nicholas Poussin
(1594–1665)

*The Baptism and Temptation of
Christ,* French Psalter of
Ingeburg, c.1210

Temptation of Christ, Très
Riches Heures du Duc de Berry,
early fifteenth century

*The Miraculous Draught of
Fishes,* from a choir book, by
Zanobi di Benedetto Strozzi
(1412–68)

The Marriage at Cana
by Gerard David (c.1460–1523)

The Sermon on the Mount by Fra Angelico (c.1387–1455)

Christ Preaching on the Sea of Galilee by Jan Brueghel the Elder (1568–1625)

Christ Walking on the Waves, from an illuminated copy of *Meditations on the Life of Christ* by St. Bonaventure, mid-fourteenth-century

The Good Samaritan by Cornelis Cornelisz van Haarlem (1562–1638)

The Prodigal Son by Hieronymus Bosch (c.1450–1516)

"Suffer the little children to come unto me, and forbid them not" by Reverend James Willis (fl.1740–77)

The Raising of Lazarus by the Master of Coetivy (fl. 1450–75)

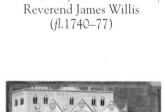

The Raising of Lazarus and *The Entry of Christ into Jerusalem,* Psalter of Ingeberg, c.1210

The Cleansing of the Temple by Ambrogio Bondone Giotto (c.1266–1337)

Maesta: Entry in Jerusalem by Duccio di Buoninsegna (c.1278–1318)

The Last Supper by Fra Angelico (c. 1387–1455)

Last Supper from a predella panel entitled *The Lamentation of Christ* by Joos Van Cleve (*c.*1485–1540/41)

Agony in the Garden by Andrea Mantegna (1431–1506)

The Arrest of Jesus by Fra Angelico (c. 1387–1455)

Road to Calvary by Simone Martini (1284–1344)

Crucifixion by the Boucicaut Master, The Chevalier Hours, early fifteenth century

The Deposition from the *Descent from the Cross* series by Rogier van der Weyden (1399–1464)

The Crucifixion, from Missal written for Cardinal Oliviero Carafa, Archbishop of Naples, 1488

Noli Me Tangere by Fra Angelico (*c.*1387–1455)

The Apostles Leaving the Virgin to Spread the Word of Christ by Jean Colombe (*fl.*1467–1529), Très Riches Heures du Duc de Berry

The Ascension of Christ by Pietro Perugino (c.1445–1523)

For Chi Hyon Boyce

A note on the text from the author

In retelling the life of Jesus, I have selectively chosen events from the Gospels of the
New Testament – Matthew, Mark, Luke and John. The sources I used were the Holy Bible in the
King James version and the Revised Standard version, a Meridian book, published by the
Penguin Group, copyright 1962 by the World Publishing Co.

Published by the Penguin Group
Penguin Putnam Inc., 375 Hudson Street, New York, New York 10014, USA
Penguin Books Ltd, 27 Wrights Lane, London W8 5TZ, England
Penguin Books Australia Ltd, Ringwood, Victoria, Australia
Penguin Books Canada Ltd, 10 Alcorn Avenue, Toronto, Ontario, Canada M4V 3B2
Penguin Books (NZ) Ltd, 182-190 Wairau Road, Auckland 10, New Zealand
Penguin Books Ltd, Registered Offices: Harmondsworth, Middlesex, England

First published in Great Britain by Viking, 1998
First published in U.S.A. by Viking, a member of Penguin Putnam Inc., 1998

3 5 7 9 10 8 6 4 2

Text copyright © Mary Pope Osborne, 1998
All rights reserved.

ISBN 0-670-87313-6
Library of Congress Catalog Card Number: 98–60316
Set in Goudy
Printed in Belgium by Proost

The publisher would like to thank the Bridgeman Art Library, London/New York and the following for their kind
permission to reproduce works of art: Agnew & Sons, London: 16. British Library, London: 6, 10, 13, 37. Christian
Museum, Esztergom: 15. Christie's Images: 25 (top). City of Bristol Museum and Art Gallery: 5. Coram Foundation,
London: 28 (top). Corpus Christi College, Oxford: 25 (bottom). Fitzwilliam Museum, University of Cambridge: 38 (top).
Johnny van Haeften Gallery, London: 26. Lambeth Palace Library, London: 17 (top). Louvre, Paris: 17 (bottom), 21,
28 and 29 (bottom), 36. Musée des Beaux-Arts, Lyons: 43. Musée Condé, Chantilly, France: 11, 18, 19, 29 (top) and
30 (top), 42. Musée Jacquemart-André, Paris: 7. Museo dell'Opera del Duomo, Siena: 31. Museo di San Marco
dell' Angelico, Florence: 12, 20, 23, 32 (bottom), 35, 41. Museum Boymans van Beuningen, Rotterdam: 27. National
Gallery, London: 9, 34. Osma-Soria Chapter House, Soria: 14 (top). Osterreichische Nationalbibliothek, Vienna: 8.
Palazzo Pitti, Florence: 3 and 14 (bottom). Prado, Madrid: 38 and 39. Scrovegni (Arena) Chapel, Padua: 30 (bottom).
We would also like to thank the Louvre, Paris and Service Photographique de la Réunion des Musées Nationaux, Paris
for permission to reproduce the painting on pages 32 and 33 (top). Photo RMN – Gérard Blot.